God's Touch Among The Amish
Book 3

Book 3

Sorrowful yet always rejoicing…
An Amish woman's true story of how
Jesus touched her life.

By
Miriam Fisher

xulon PRESS

Copyright © 2012 by Aaron Jay Beiler

God's Touch Among The Amish, Book 3
by Miriam Fisher

Printed in the United States of America

ISBN 9781624191886

Unless otherwise indicated, Bible quotations are taken from The King James Version of the Bible.

Cover design: Grant Elrod
Editing: Frank Testa

www.xulonpress.com

Table Of Contents

Table Of Contents

Endorsements

When I think of my dear friend Miriam Fisher and the school of Christ that she has been enrolled in these past twenty-some years, these verses come to mind: *"For thy Maker is thine husband; the LORD of hosts is his name; and thy Redeemer the Holy One of Israel; the God of the whole earth shall he be called. For the LORD hath called thee as a woman forsaken and grieved in spirit, and a wife of youth, when thou wast refused, saith thy God. For a small moment have I forsaken thee; but with great mercies will I gather thee."* These verses are a picture of Miriam's life. She daily walks a difficult road, but our loving Father surrounds her with His tender mercies, and those of us around her are also the glad recipients of these mercies as they flow through her into our lives. Christ's sweet Spirit channeled through her earthen vessel is a continual tribute to His grace, *"...that the power may be of God, and not of us. We are troubled on every side, yet not distressed; we are perplexed, but not in despair; persecuted, but not forsaken; cast down, but not destroyed; always bearing about in the body the dying of the Lord Jesus, that the life also of Jesus might be made manifest in our body."*

Although Miriam was not able to bear children, she has many children in the faith who "arise up and call her blessed." There are many who consider her a close friend and confidante – many whose heartaches she takes faithfully to the throne of grace as a true prayer warrior. Her continual suffering enables her to share the burdens of others from the depths of her own tender heart. I once read that, although many virtues of Christ can be imitated to some degree, the virtue of compassion can come only from an intimate abiding in Jesus. It is this compassion of Christ flowing through Miriam that so lifts my spirit as I fellowship with her. So often looking back over meaningful time spent with her I think of the verse *"Rejoice with them that rejoice; weep with them that weep."* She is quick to shed tears over my sorrows. She abides in the Balm of Gilead and it shows. As we bare our hearts to one another, God is faithful time and again to give us garments of praise for the spirit of heaviness. It is sweet to cry together, but sweeter yet to praise Him together.

During difficult periods in my life I have sometimes felt the need of the help and prayer of others yet lacked the courage to call someone with whom to share. At those times I have cried out to my Father, asking Him to move someone to contact me if it is His will for someone to do so. In several of these instances, it has been Miriam who has been moved by His Spirit to reach out to me. Her closeness to Jesus is used to minister to the Body of Christ. Surely the Lord uses her suffering to keep her humble and broken as she imparts Jesus to those with whom she has to do. She is a much beloved daughter of the King active in the furtherance of His kingdom, and it is her passionate longing that God receive glory from her life.

Hearts will be strengthened and faith renewed through the reading of this testimony. Those who have endured heartache for the cause of Christ will find comfort and encouragement as they read of His faithfulness in the life of Miriam Fisher. To God be the glory!

Sarah Barnard

My heart was touched in a renewed way as I read Miriam's journey. It brought back memories as I walked with my sister through this life-changing event of forsaking those nearest and dearest to follow Christ, the new found joy in her life. Miriam has a marvelous testimony of the effects of the cross of Christ inwrought in her life through hardship. Out of all the heart wrenching experiences including dealing with physical pain due to her medical history of the past she is a testimony of Christ revealing Himself through her life and is a inspiration to many of Gods love and compassion being perfected through her pain and suffering. Amazing grace how sweet and precious; this testimony will encourage others in their unfavorable situations in their quest for God.

Katie Fisher

Sister Miriam's testimony of searching for life and her walk of faith is inspiring. Her life is an example in accordance with the book of Acts. It's one of struggle, persecution, and sometimes loneliness for the outward man. But it also speaks of peace, joy, and love in the inward man, which is the grace of God to everyone that believeth. Yea, all that live godly in Christ Jesus shall suffer persecution!

Bro. Emanuel Esh

What an inspiring story of a challenging journey. Knowing Miriam while she was walking through these experiences, I realized that she totally lived a surrendered life to Jesus. Many people when faced with adversities like Miriam has, would question and even turn away from Jesus, Miriam chose the better way and pressed in to Him. A great story for those who are caught up in the 'spirit of religiosity'.

Friend & neighbor of Miriam for 20 years
Linda L. Eberly

Through the grace of the Lord Jesus Christ, Miriam Fisher has been able to remain in the joy of the Lord while passing through many trials and afflictions. As you read her testimony you will be encouraged to fully follow Christ and be assured that in spite of great trials you can be more than a conquer in Him.

Arise in the grace of Christ, and say with Apostle Paul, I can do all things through Christ who strengthens me.

Aaron Jay Beiler

As sorrowful , yet alway rejoicing ; as poor, yet making many rich ; as having nothing, and yet possessing all things. 2 Corinthians 6:10

Chapter 1

Challenged from My Youth

*Jesus saith unto him, I am the
way, the truth, and the life: no man
cometh unto the Father, but by me."
John 14:6*

On a spring day in April, 1975, the truth of the
words in John 14:6 became reality to me in a
way that really changed my life.

I was born and raised in Lancaster County, PA,
in an Old Order Amish home, the second youngest
of eight children – four sisters and three brothers.
Growing up on an Amish farm, my childhood was
that of a typical happy child, until around age 11
when I experienced times of not feeling well, with
fatigue and loss of energy. My parents tried every-
thing to help me. They took me to a family doctor
who described it as a matter of my nerves, and then
they tried homeopathic doctors. I would feel better
for a while, but over two years my condition grew
worse. My parents felt it had to be more than nerves

or ordinary childhood laziness and decided to seek further medical advice.

In December, 1965, on my thirteenth birthday, I was admitted to Lancaster General Hospital. It wasn't the most exciting way to celebrate my entry into my teen years, but it gave me a hope that help would be found to make me feel better. I did not realize it would be 21 days later before I would get back home. The doctors discovered I had a brain tumor, and on the tenth day I underwent surgery. Most of the time I was brave but it was a difficult time for me. The one day when my parents came I was having a test done which seemed to take very long. When I came back to my room after the test it was time for my parents to leave for home and I didn't get to spend time with them; I remember that day I had to cry. Though the tumor was not cancerous, it pressed on the pituitary gland or master gland that controls other major glands. As a result of the surgery to remove the brain tumor, the pituitary gland was destroyed and I was told I would be on medication for the rest of my life. I was already small of stature, but now I stopped growing physically. After the surgery, as a young teen, I was shocked to see all the hair removed from the front of my head. My dad suggested wearing a wig for a time, but I didn't like that idea and my hair grew back quickly.

Because of the complications with my pituitary gland not working, I had some new issues to deal with. For several years, right up to the time I was married, I went numerous times to Johns Hopkins Hospital in Baltimore, Maryland, spending a week or more at a time going through tests to monitor how I responded to certain medications. One of my parents would stay at a place nearby the hospital during those times. I was put on some growth hormone for a while that my dad injected, and I grew about six inches taller.

I had a tremendous family that showed me a lot of love. My parents were so special in caring for me. My brothers and sisters were a big support to me during those hard times. I also had a wonderful teacher, Mr. Shurr, who would come once a week to tutor me at home where I did school work until I was able to return to school.

All that I experienced through surgery, hospital stays, medical treatments, and my physical condition, made me feel inferior at times to other youth. But through it all, I began to think seriously about life, and especially about God, and I really desired to live my life in a right way.

Chapter 2

A Young Member of the Amish Church

At age sixteen, I was baptized and became a member of the Amish Church. I really did not understand the true meaning of baptism and I didn't know anything about being born "of water and of the Spirit" as Jesus said was necessary to "enter into the kingdom of God". (John 3:5) I certainly did not know what it meant to be "born again" – to repent and commit my whole life in faith to Jesus Christ. Baptism was just the expected thing to do in the Amish Church when you reached a certain age. I wanted to do what the church and my parents expected of me.

At this time, as was customary; I became part of a youth group. Though it wasn't as "wild" as some Amish youth groups, I knew I was involved in some things that my parents and the church would not really approve of. Sorry to say, the way we dressed and meeting the standards of the church seemed more important than sinful practices including "bed-courtship" (couples sleeping together before actual marriage) .

My religious life consisted in praying memorized prayers that my parents had taught me, or prayers from a prayer book. I seemed to have a form of godliness without any real life or personal relationship with the Lord. I was religious but I was not redeemed by Jesus' blood. I found myself praying a short prayer: "Forgive me for what I did wrong, help me to do better, and take me to heaven someday." I would pray that prayer night after night. That was the only prayer I remember saying from the heart. I believe God heard my sincere prayer, and some years later He drew me to Himself and showed me my need for a Savior and salvation through Jesus Christ. He would take away the blindness of my heart, and I would come to say, "I see the light"- the light that comes from Jesus Christ who is the Light.

Chapter 3

"For Better or For Worse"

I met my husband at the Amish youth group we both were part of. We married in November, 1972, one day before I turned 20. We moved onto my husband's home farm, which for me took a lot of adjusting to. Even though we had our good times together, my life as a married woman was not all what I had expected it to be and all I had longed for. In longing for a closer relationship with my husband, I made a lot of mistakes in trying to be the wife I needed to be. I felt unloved, and also I had to deal with the fact of not being able to have any children of our own because of the destruction of my pituitary gland during my brain tumor surgery.

The Loss of My Dad

In 1974, while I was still in the midst of these life struggles, and about a year and a half after marriage, my dad, at age 58, died very suddenly at work of a heart attack. He, along with my mother, had been a big support to me over the time of my sickness as a child, my surgery and early months of my marriage. Dad had tried to be of help with repair work where we lived, and gave words of encouragement when he knew I was struggling with some of my circumstances.

And now, all of a sudden, I was left without my dad. He was so much a part of my life because of his involvement in the sickness and trials of my youth, and it was hard to believe he would not be there for me as he had been. Yet, somehow, there was grace and courage to continue on in life. As much as I missed my dad, and grieved over the loss of his presence with us, I realized I needed to reach out to my precious mother who was hurting more than I was. Comforting and reaching out to her seemed to bring healing to my own heart.

Chapter 4

A Move of God in My Family

About this time, and a little before my dad's death, our family began to experience other changes and circumstances. One of my sisters was fighting depression. She was in a intense struggle in her search for God and for genuine peace within her heart. She went to my dad before he died to ask for forgiveness for disobeying him in her earlier years. Dad told her he had already forgiven her. She had read a book by David Wilkerson, about events he predicted would happen in the end times. She would read the book, put it aside, and then be drawn back to it again. It brought her under conviction, knowing she was not ready to meet the Lord. She would say, "If I only knew I'm saved!" In the Amish religion we were taught you cannot know if you are saved and your sins are forgiven, we only hope. They believed if we abide by the traditions of the Amish, we can only hope to get to heaven. They would teach that it is wrong to say you know you are forgiven and saved; thinking that a person who says that is proud. I remember telling my sister, "I don't think we can know if we are saved until we reach heaven." How deceived I was. My sister experienced a time of depression for approximately a half year, until she came to faith in Christ and experienced the "new birth".

My sister had a friend, who along with her husband, was born again, and had left the Amish traditions. She would call her friend, and her friend would explain to her what salvation through Christ really is. She prayed with her a number of times. At first, she could not grasp what it meant to be born again. But one day, while reading an article on the new birth, she realized there was nothing she could do to be saved, except by faith to believe in Jesus Christ and what He did at the cross in giving His life for her. Now she had faith and became born again! "Jesus answered, and said unto him, Verily, verily, I say unto thee, Except a man be born again, he cannot see the kingdom of God." John 3:3

At first she would share what God had done in her heart, and how she believed you can know if you are born again. When she realized we as a family were not really receiving what she was saying, and in some ways thought she was wrong and was being deceived, she decided to keep quiet, and live her new walk with Christ before us. She, along with her family, lived right next door to our mother, so when we went to see our mom, we would usually see her, too. My sister definitely had changed; she was no longer this depressed person who hadn't seemed to watch over her children, she had now been set free. She had a burden that others, too, might come to know Jesus Christ as their only hope for salvation. She desired that others might see that it is "Not by works of righteousness that we have done, but according to His mercy He saved us, by the washing of regeneration, and renewing of the Holy Ghost which He shed on us abundantly through Jesus Christ our Savior: That being justified by His grace, we should be made heirs according to the hope of eternal life." Titus 3: 5-7

I thought my sister was being deceived and I was afraid she would leave the Amish religion. Having been taught that it is wrong to leave the Amish traditions, I would try to show her where she was wrong. I would remind her of the Scriptures the Amish would often use when someone would be thinking of leaving the Amish religion.

More Family Members Turn to Jesus

Around the same time that my sister was going through her experience, my youngest brother also came to see his need of Jesus Christ. At the time of my dad's death he was the only sibling still living at home. Before my dad died, my brother was going through a time of rebellion toward my parents. He was not a member of the Amish but my parents did not approve of him having a car and of his drinking. One day before he died, my dad tried to admonish my brother, but my brother did not want to listen to and rebelliously walked away from dad, slamming the door behind him. The next day when my brother heard that dad dropped over dead, he was devastated, feeling he was responsible and the cause of our dad's death.

As a young teenager of 18 living his wild life, he knew he had to change the lifestyle he had been living. He started to drive his horse and buggy again, and tried to quit drinking. He soon found that in himself he was powerless, and it wasn't long before he was back to his old ways. During this time, a person he worked with shared Jesus Christ with him. My brother gave his life to Christ, asking for forgiveness for his sins, and Christ changed him. His desire to live the life he used to live was immediately taken away. There was no doubt that something had happened in his heart.

"Therefore, if any man be in Christ, he is a new creature: old things are passed away: behold all things are become new." 2 Corinthians 5:17 Since Henry was not a member of the Amish religion, it seemed easier for him to leave, which he soon did, and connected with a Christian church.

Within that year, two more of my sisters came to see that salvation is by faith in Jesus Christ alone, and that one must be born again to spend eternity with Jesus in heaven. They accepted the gift of salvation though Jesus and the blood He shed at the cross. I began to ponder all that was happening in my family. I would question myself: "What is truth? Which church is right?" Again and again, the Lord brought to my mind this Scripture: "Jesus sayeth unto him, I am the way, the truth, and the life: no man cometh unto the Father, but by me." John 145:6

God seemed to be showing me that salvation is not in a church, it is in Jesus alone. "Neither is there salvation in any other: for there is none other name given among men whereby we must be saved." Acts 4:12

My heart was opening more and more to the realization that my family members, who had come to accept the Lord Jesus and His finished work on the cross, having a relationship with Christ, were not on the wrong path.

Facing My Own Self-righteousness

I began to think that maybe there was something that I needed a better understanding of, and maybe I had been self-righteous, thinking that if I dressed and did things the way the Amish religion stressed, I would get to heaven based on that. I had to see that my righteousness was as "filthy rags". (Isaiah 64: 6) I had to see that I was indeed lost and as much in need of a Savior as the drunkards and harlots on the streets. In Matthew 21:31, Jesus said to the religious people: "Verily I say unto you, that the publicans and the harlots go into the kingdom of God before you." It seems that the publicans and harlots know they are lost and need a Savior and come to Jesus before those who do not see their lost-ness because of their own self-righteous deeds. And more than anything else, that is what I needed to be saved from. I was self-righteous! I thought I was alright; I read my Bible. I prayed out of a prayer book, and dressed the way I was expected to. I knew About Jesus, yet I did not know Him! There is a great difference in knowing about Him, and knowing Him in a personal way.

Chapter 5

I Needed and Accepted Jesus

On a spring day in April 1975, one of my sisters
came to spend the day with me at my house.
She came to help me do some cleaning, but little did I
know that morning that the biggest help she would be
to me would not be in cleaning the house, but rather
in a spiritual cleaning in myself. My heart was open
to truth and she realized that, and we talked. I don't
remember all that we talked about, but I remember
her telling me we need to accept Jesus Christ as our
Savior, we need to have a personal relationship with
Him. When she told me that, it was as if a light went
on in my soul. I knew I did not have a personal relationship with Jesus Christ, and had never in faith per-
sonally accepted Him as my Savior, or accepted His
forgiveness for my sins. I had never committed my
life to Him, going to the cross in a personal way for
myself. That was the day that I opened my heart to
the Lord Jesus. That spring day, I asked Him into my
heart, realizing He is the way, and He died for me.
Yet, for a few weeks I struggled with really being
assured of my salvation.

Assured of Salvation

I knew as I read the Scriptures that it was not wrong to know I was saved, as I had been taught in the Amish teachings. "He that believeth on the Son of God hath the witness in himself: he that believeth not God hath made Him a liar; because he believeth not the record that God gave of His Son. And this is the record, that God hath given to us eternal life, and this life is in His Son. He that hath the Son hath life, and he that hath not the Son of God, hath not life. These things have I written unto you that believe on the name of the Son of God: that ye may know that ye have eternal life and that ye may believe on the name of the Son of God." 1 John 5:10-13 "The Spirit itself beareth witness with our spirit, that we are the children of God." Romans 8:16 These Scriptures seemed to tell me I should know, if I believe God, and His Spirit would give me the witness and assurance that I was saved. Praise the Lord, He did! He gave a peace I could not explain. Jesus said, "Peace I leave with you, My peace I give unto you: not as the world giveth, give I unto you. Let not your heart be troubled, neither let it be afraid." John 14:27 In Paul's Epistle to the Philippians, we read about "the peace of God which passeth all understanding". And He does give a peace beyond what we understand.

And as that peace and assurance of salvation became a reality, it was hard to stay quiet. I had received a GIFT and I wanted others also to experience the GIFT of salvation through Jesus Christ. As I shared my faith with my family and friends, there were those who did not understand, and this brought opposition; it was not an altogether easy path but God did not promise our life would all be easy. He promised grace and He gave the Holy Spirit to guide and to teach. It was good to face opposition, for it caused me to search the Scriptures to see what was truth.

Facing Opposition

My sisters who were still in the Amish Church, yet born again, along with a few others, started meeting together for Bible study and prayer. I joined them for a few times until my husband asked me not to go to the meetings. I wanted to submit to him, so I did not join the prayer group again. As time went on, my fellowship with other believers was very limited. I was asked not to talk to my born again sisters, their families, or anyone who believed like we did. To me, that meant all born again believers.

I had a non-Amish Christian neighbor I would talk with on rare occasions, for I knew I was being watched. Yet, God was faithful to me through it all. At that time of my life, I had a cleaning job near a post office. I felt God laid it on my heart to get a post office box. He knew I was desperate for real true Christian communication with my born again family and friends. It came to be a tremendous blessing to me. One day a week, when I went to my cleaning job, I anticipated receiving some encouraging letters from my sisters and friends. That encouraged me to spiritually and emotionally survive! Praise the Lord!

Need for Fellowship

I longed to have more true Christian fellowship. Sometimes I longed to just see someone who was one in heart and faith with me. There were times I felt like I was in a prison, and the Lord reminded me of the account in the Bible when Paul and Silas were in prison and how they prayed and sang praises to God. (Acts 16: 25) As I chose to do the same, God was truly there to strengthen me, and I was encouraged. I came across a poem entitled, "Along the Shores of Loneliness", written by a woman who experienced loneliness, and talked of it being a time alone, away from her friends, and it seemed to be like being in a desert. Yet, in the midst of the desert she found a flower growing, and the name of the flower was "God is enough". I, too, experienced that no matter what we may face, even in those alone times, God is enough to meet my deepest need. It was a time I truly learned to cry out to God in prayer. I really cried out from the depths of my heart, because I needed Him, and I knew I needed Him. I knew that I could not make it on my own strenght. *"...t'was on the shores of loneliness that I really learned to pray. No more the hurried whisper to 'bless the road I trod,' but the anguished cry of a broken soul who needed more of God." ("Along the Shores of Loneliness" poem)* Those times all alone with God taught me that nothing satisfies my inner longings like being alone with Jesus. The cross truly is bitter and sweet at the same time. Bitter, because it brings death to my self-life, my flesh, and yet sweet, because the Lord's presence is sweeter. "O taste and see that the Lord is good: blessed is the man that trusteth in him." Psalm 34:8 "Thou wilt show me the path of life: in thy presence is fullness of joy: at thy right hand there are pleasures for evermore." Psalm 16:11

The Psalms would minister life to me many times as I prayed and poured out my heart to the Lord. I cried out to God for guidance and direction for my life; asking Him to not let me do anything out of rebellion toward those who opposed me, but that all I did would be done out of a love for my Savior, the One who first loved me and gave His life for me.

Chapter 6

Excommunication

What a joy to my heart when one of my friends at the Amish church began opening up her heart to me in her search for truth. Then, in December, 1982, she and her husband were excommunicated from the Amish religion since they had started attending another church. It was expected by the Amish church that I, along with everyone else, would agree to excommunicate them. But these were my Christian friends, how could I truthfully, as a born again believer, shun them?! I knew in all honesty I could not. In January, 1983, I was told by the church leaders I would need to make a confession in the church for not giving my agreement to excommunicate my friends. I was given a certain amount of time to consider whether I would confess or not. And if I would not confess, I was told something would happen to me. I was not told what would happen, but I knew it meant excommunication for me.

I cried out to God for grace and strength to do what He wanted me to do. At one point I could not see any way through, and I had thoughts of confessing I had done wrong when I had not given my agreement to excommunicate them. But in my heart, I knew I had only been honest, and God expected me to be honest and truthful. I felt so alone and misunderstood. My heart was in turmoil and not at peace. The Lord brought me to His Word: "For by thy words thou shalt be justified and by thy words thou shalt be condemned." Matthew 12:37. I once again surrendered all to God, telling Him I would speak the truth and leave the consequences to Him. Bible verses like these would be my strength: "The Lord is my light, and my salvation, whom shall I fear? The Lord is the strength of my life, of whom shall I be afraid." Psalm 27:1 "In God have I put my trust, I will not be afraid what man can do unto me." Psalm 56:11

I read an article that brought out the importance of being faithful to God. What left a great impact on my heart is when it mentioned about how we talk about the cost of following Christ, yet have we considered the cost of NOT following Christ! After reading the article, I was greatly challenged concerning the consequence if I would draw back and not fully obey God. I realized that some day I would stand before God and give an account of my life. I understood that the cost of following Christ would spare me from the consequences and the cost of NOT following Christ. I decided to follow Christ no matter how much pain it cost me.

In March 1983, I was asked to come to church and confess that I did wrong in not giving my agreement to the excommunication, and also for listening to a sermon tape. The thought of being in front of the whole church seemed scary to me. I knew that I was considered rebellious, yet all I wanted was to be true to the God who had become so real to me. I asked other believers to pray for me. And the Lord gave me a verse when I went to church that Sunday morning: "Thou wilt keep him in perfect peace whose mind is stayed on thee because he trusteth in Thee." Isaiah 26:3 God was reminding me if I kept my focus on Jesus, He would give me perfect peace. He was true to His promise! I was amazed by the calm and peace in my heart. I knew it was not me, it was God in me. There were people praying for me, and I felt the power of their prayers. The Amish leaders questioned and challenged me before the church members for close to two hours. And it ended up by them telling me I had six more weeks to reconsider confessing. I went home with mixed feelings. I knew what was ahead if I stayed true to God. It seemed like a long journey; my heart was heavy and weary and I desired to have it all over with.

Chapter 7

"Like a Bird Set Free Out of Its Cage"

W hen the six weeks ended, I was asked if I still believed the same, to which I answered, "Yes", and I was excommunicated. I went home that day free in my heart, like a bird set free out of its cage! Yet, I also knew my faith came with a cost. There would be those of my own family and friends, who I greatly loved and were dear to my heart, which would now shun and reject me. My heart hurt, and I felt I was the cause of their hurt.

It hurt to be misunderstood and rejected, but it caused me to draw nearer to God. I would cry my many tears to Him. My heart was burdened for my loved ones, desiring they would come to salvation through faith in Christ. I knew this was God allowing me to be excommunicated and shunned. This was His way of telling me to come out of the Amish religion and follow Christ with all my heart.

We lived on a farm, and many times in the middle of the night, with a burdened heart, I would walk back and forth in our farm lane weeping and crying out to God. I asked God, "Is this really what You had in mind when you asked me to follow You?" God seemed to say to me, "You follow Me, and I will take care of you." And He always has! He is so faithful! Those times with God were so precious!

I committed myself to remain faithful in my marriage and to sincerely love my husband even though he supported the Amish leaders decision to excommunicate me. God did not say my life would be all easy, but He did say "in the world ye shall have tribulation, but be of good cheer; I have overcome the world." John 16: 33 "Wherein ye greatly rejoiced, though now for a season, if need be ye are in heaviness through manifold temptations; that the trial of your faith being much more precious than of gold that perisheth, though it be tried with fire, might be found unto praise and honor and glory at the appearing of Jesus Christ." 1 Peter 1: 6-7

Following Christ is not all easy; our broken hearts and trials can bring us closer to Christ, so that we can experience more of His grace, His love, and His strength. And that is my heart's cry: to be drawn closer to our Heavenly Father. "That I may know Him and the power of His resurrection, and the fellowship of His sufferings." Philippians 3:10

Now that I was not a member of the Amish religion anymore, I felt that God was directing me to fellowship with other believers of like precious faith. "Not forsaking the assembling of ourselves together as the manner of some is: but exhorting one another, and so much the more, as ye see the day approaching." Hebrews 10: 25. It wasn't long before I started attending Charity Christian Fellowship. I so well remember the first time I went to Charity. The preacher preached about counting the cost of being a disciple of Christ, from Luke 14:28. It seemed to me that the message was just for me; it greatly ministered to me.

Although I was excommunicated, twice a month I continued to go with my husband to the Amish Church, I went with him for about two more years then I began to realize my husband did not want me to go with him anymore if I wasn't planning to go back to the Amish as a member. Because of a certain situation, I sensed God telling me this certain Sunday would be the last time I go to the Amish Church; I went through a battle at the thought of not coming back. As I was sitting in the church, I kept thinking of Jesus in the Garden of Gethsemane, and how He seemed to struggle, and then said to His Father, "Not as I will, but as Thou wilt." And my heart also said, "Not my will, but Thine." The hardest part in not coming back was that my husband still went to the Amish Church. Yet, I knew I was no longer my own, I was bought with a price – the precious blood of Jesus and I must follow Him faithfully.

Burden for My People

Along with my sisters, I had great burden for others, especially the Amish who were not born again. We started having prayer meetings with others joining us for prayer. Sometimes we had a whole room of people carrying the same vision and deep burden on

33

their hearts for a move of God in Lancaster County. We cried and prayed that God would bring a mighty spiritual revival among the Amish; that God would open up the hearts of the Amish to the truth and salvation. It was so special to me to be able to gather with others, and to cry out to God together. It was a longing of my heart being fulfilled.

In my earlier years while attending Charity Church, we had revival meetings there for an evangelist from Ohio. Through the powerful preaching and conviction of the Holy Spirit, my own heart, along with that of many others, was cleansed in a deeper way and greatly revived. A few Amish families, along with two of my sisters' husbands came and received Jesus Christ as their Savior, giving their lives to Him. What joy, what rejoicing! Now we had some more joining us in prayer, for there were still others in need of turning their lives over to Christ. We kept on intensely praying and crying tears to God. "They that sow in tears shall reap in joy." Psalms 126:5

As I journey on with the Lord Jesus, He has become a Friend to me. I could not make it through life without Him! In the midst of my joys, sorrows, failures, valleys and storms of life, His grace and faithfulness have come through for me time and time again. He is my rock, my shield, my fortress, my shepherd. In sorrow He is my comfort and my joy, and in weakness He is my strength. "But they that wait upon the Lord shall renew their strength: they shall mount up with wings as eagles: they shall run, and not be weary: and they shall walk, and not faint." Isaiah 40:31

Chapter 8

Gods Faithfulness

During one of my times, when I found myself becoming weary, weary of serving in my home, I was talking to God and asking Him, "How can I keep on giving and giving, when it seems that I receive nothing in return? (I felt unloved, unappreciated, rejected in my own home.) God told me, "My storehouse never gets dry, never becomes empty. As long as you give, I will give you something to give." Again I surrendered my heart, and God faithfully met my need. God is so good! He is always true to His Word. "O, the depth of the riches both of the wisdom and the knowledge of God. How unsearchable are His judgments, and His ways passed finding out!" Romans 11:33

At another time, as I came home from a weekend away with some of my Christian friends from church, I was longing for a welcome home, but I did not receive any. Over the next few days I struggled with unforgiveness and feelings of becoming bitter. God in His mercy had someone send me a note. This person had no way of knowing the battles I was facing in my mind, except by the Spirit of God. In part, the note read: "In prayer I had an overwhelming compulsion to ask you to read carefully the following two verses: 'To sum up, let all be harmonious, sympathetic, brotherly, kindhearted, and humble in spirit; not returning evil for evil, or insult for insult, but giving a blessing instead; for you were called in the very purpose that you might inherit a blessing.' 1 Peter 3: 8-9. God wants you to forgive and bless someone who hurt you in the past. Perhaps recently! You and I can release great joy and peace in ourselves when we forgive. We must not return evil for evil, insult for insult. Forgive! And He promises you will be blessed. Hold no grudges! Let no root of bitterness spring up – it will choke you!" Wow! It was as if the note came directly from God for me! Needless to say, I dropped on my knees and cried out to God in repentance and surrendered my hurts and bitter feelings. And again His peace flooded my heart. God's love is so great even in our failure. He reaches out in redemption to restore His peace and joy no matter what the circumstances when there is repentance.

I love my God because He first loved me, and gave Himself for me. I read a quote one time: "Life isn't always fair: but neither was the cross. Jesus took that cross as an instrument of execution, and transformed it into the hope of the world. He will do that with your cross, too, if you will let Him." Robert Russell. We are promised that "all things work together for good to them that love God, to them who are the called according to His purpose." Romans 8:28 It brings a rest to my heart in seeing all God allows in my life is for His divine purpose.

The Example of Joseph

Joseph has been one of my favorite Bible characters. He was mistreated by his brothers; sold into slavery, falsely accused, put into prison, and seemingly forgotten in prison. Yet, it appears he showed no resentment, but rather went through it with patience. And when his brothers came to him in their time of need, he showed no revenge, but instead he forgave. Because he was where God had allowed him to be, he was able to save his family who were so desperately in need. Joseph told his brothers, "But as for you, you thought evil against me, but God meant it for good, to bring to pass, as it is this day, to save much people alive." Genesis 50:20 God, even today, places his children in unique circumstances at times, and what our enemy desires to use for evil, God will turn around for good if our lives are surrendered to Him. Though, in my journey with the Lord, my life has had its share of trials and sufferings, I count it a great grace and privilege to be a born again follower of Jesus Christ. God's Word tells us: " For I reckon that the sufferings of this present time are not worthy to be compared with the glory which shall be revealed in us." Romans 8:18

Loving with God's Love

It is amazing how a heart at times can hold sorrow

and joy at the same time! I can truly say, "The joy of the Lord is my strength." Nehemiah 8:10 "Who shall separate us from the love of Christ? Shall tribulation, or distress, or persecution, or famine, or nakedness, or peril, or sword? Nay, in all these things we are more than conquerors through Him who loved us." Romans 8:35,37. God's love is so great!

I am so thankful that God opened my heart to His love, His truth, and I, in response, opened my heart to Him, and chose to follow Him. I would never want to go back to my old life, when I walked in darkness. God shows Himself strong in the hard times. He knows what he yet wants to do in my life. And I desire with all my heart to let Him have His way. He is worthy! God has enabled me to remain in my marriage and to accept suffering in peace and be sustained by Jesus. - I have been greatly comforted by Isaiah 54, (especially verse 5), "For thy maker is thine husband: the Lord of hosts is his name: and thy Redeemer the Holy One of Israel: the God of the whole earth shall he be called."

Have Faith in God

God has a plan and purpose for each one's life on this earth. No matter what you may be facing in your life, Jesus calls to you. "Come unto Me all ye that labor and are heavy laden, and I will give you rest. Take My yoke upon you, and learn of Me, for I am meek and lowly in heart; and ye shall find rest unto your souls." Matthew 11: 28-29 He is the only one who can fill that emptiness in our hearts, and He is longing that all will come to Him. He came to give us "beauty for ashes, the oil of joy for mourning, the garment of praise for the spirit of heaviness;" Isaiah 61:3 He is the Way, the Truth, and the Life. "Neither is there salvation in any other: for there is none other name under heaven given among men whereby we must be saved." Acts 4:12

Contact Information
Charity Christian Fellowship
717.656.4155

Miriam Fisher
717.371.0006

For book ordering:
717.351.0800

Printed in the USA
CPSIA information can be obtained
at www.ICGtesting.com
LVHW092327300724
786956LV00033B/399

9 781624 191886